New Word
A Day

Vol 6

INTRODUCTION:
Learning a new word a day is a great way to
stimulate your mind.

ISBN-13: 978-1499273137
ISBN-10: 1499273134

Get a daily word in your email.
Signup Free at NewWordADay.com.

!

He owned an anachronistic television. It is anachronistic because everyone has a flat screen now.

ANACHRONISTIC
<Anna-cron-nist-tik>
Out-of-date; archaic; dated;
Existing out of place for a certain time period.
Suspenders are anachronistic because the belt is now used to hold up pants.

ANA - CHRONISTIC

Ana	(Reminds)	Anti
Chronistic	(Reminds)	Chronicle

Memory Trick: Being anti-chronicle because it could not be in that time period.
ANTI CHRONICLE

What kind of bulge does effulge in a dark room?

I LIVE IN THE HINTERLAND,
IT'S A LONELY HABIT,
SO I'LL START A BAND,
WITH A MOUSE AND A RABBIT.

HINTERLAND
<Hint-a-land>
Outback; sticks; bush;
Existing as a country backwoods.
She lives in the hinterland and there is no
one around.

HINT - ER - LAND

Hint	(Reminds)	Hint or a little of
Land	(Reminds)	Land

Memory Trick: A hint of people lives in
this land.
HINT LAND

A light bulb does effulge in a dark room.
Effulge means to shine with an
abundance of light.

The piranha was a pariah and none of the little fish wanted to be his friend.

PARIAH
<Pah-rye-ya>
Outcast; outsider; exile;
A person that is unlikable.
The pariah was lonely until I befriended
him.

PARIAH

Pariah	(Reminds)	Piranha

Memory Trick: A piranha is a fish with no
friends.
PIRANHA

I perform an ablation on a pile of leaves.
What have I done?

The aforementioned document gave us the missing piece.

AFOREMENTIONED
<Ah-for-ment-shuned>

Past; previous; prior;
Referencing an earlier version.
We followed the aforementioned plan
and built it to the original drawings.

A - FORE - MENTIONED

Fore	(Reminds)	Before
Mentioned	(Reminds)	Mentioned

Memory Trick: It was before that we
mentioned it.
BEFORE MENTIONED

I removed the pile of leaves. Ablation
means to remove or take away.

The cat showed great equanimity and did not mind the little dog at all.

EQUANIMITY
<Ee-kwa-nim-et-tee>

Patience; calm; composure;
Possessing an evenness of
temperament.
Your equanimity is pleasing and your
anxiety is gone.

EQUA - NIMITY

Equa	(Reminds)	Equal
Animity	(Reminds)	Animosity

Memory Trick: Our kindness equals our
animosity. They are even.
EQUAL ANIMOSITY

You eat cookies made by your friend.
You say, "These are emetic!" Why does
your friend look at you funny?

The paradigm that the earth was flat went out of favor. Sales of flat earth maps went flat. Pun intended.

PARADIGM
<Par-ah-dime>

Pattern; standard; model;
Thinking the same thing.
Believing the earth is round is a paradigm
because it is a common belief.

PARA - DIGM

Para	(Reminds)	Parable or story
Digm	(Remind	Dime or decade

Memory Trick: A story changes through
the decades.

PARABLE DIME

Emetic means causing vomit.

The goose took a gander at the flower.

GANDER
<Gan-der>
Peek; glance; look;
Looking around.
I took a gander in the shop and I saw
new things.

GANDER

Gander	(Reminds)	Gander or goose

Memory Trick: A goose is curious and
takes a gander
GANDER

We are swimming. I say, "Your tact is
annoying." What will you probably do
next?

SEP 15

The sagacious cat was able to do math.
It was very impressive.

SAGACIOUS
<Sah-gay-shish>

Perceiving; keen; wise;
Being perceptive and understanding quickly.
You are sagacious and wise and you are never stupid.

SAGA - A - CIOUS

Saga	(Reminds)	Saga or a story
Cious	(Reminds)	Spacious

Memory Trick: We see a saga that is spacious because we are keen.
SAGA SPACIOUS

Stop touching me. Tact means to touch. It also means to handle something with great care and thought.

THE IMPORTUNATE BIRDS
WERE PESKY AND
ANNOYING.

IMPORTUNATE
<Im-poor-choo-nit>
Persistent; pressing; urgent;
Annoying and bothering like a pest.
His calls are importunate because he
wants to talk about unimportant things.

IMPORTUNATE

Importunate	(Like)	Unfortunate

Memory Trick: Pressing forward at an
unlucky time.
UNFORTUNATE

Do you have trepidation about going out
in tepid weather?

I KNOW A WAY I CAN COAX,
YOU TO DO STUFF FOR ME,
BRIBE YOU GOOD WITH A COKE,
WHEN YOU ARE THIRSTY.

COAX
<Cokes>
Persuade; manipulate; tend;
Convincing someone to act on
something.
I will coax her into completing it by telling
her the facts.

COAX

Coax	(Reminds)	Cokes

Memory Trick: We give them cokes to
persuade them to do something.
COKES

No! Tepid means warm. Trepidation
means to have fear.

The topic of birds is germane to the topic of bees because they both fly.

GERMANE
<Germ-main>
Pertinent; akin; relevant;
Relating with common bond.
Your idea is germane and it matches to
the topic.

GERM - MANE

Germ	(Reminds)	Germ or very small
Mane	(Reminds)	Main

Memory Trick: Germs are the main
relation when things are close.
GERM MAIN

You see a man standing on a dado. He
ignores you. Why does he not talk to
you?

The irksome woman would spit when she talked.

IRKSOME
<Erk-sum>

Pesky; tedious; bothersome;
Causing frustration and apprehension.
The irksome bird fled and the incessant
chirping stopped.

IRK - SOME

Irk	(Reminds)	Jerk
Some	(Reminds)	Sometimes

Memory Trick: Jerks are sometimes
annoying.
JERK SOMETIMES

He is a statue. A dado is the pedestal
that a statue stands on.

The persnickety boy would only wear fancy expensive sneakers.

PERSNICKETY
<Per-snik-et-tee>

Picky; fussy; finicky;
Being hard to please.
The persnickety cannot make up their
mind about choosing colors.

PERS - NICKETY

Pers	(Reminds)	Purse lips
Nickety	(Reminds)	Picky

Memory Trick: We purse our lips when
we are picky.
PURSE PICKY

We will dine wherever your caprice takes
us. You don't own a car. Where do we
go?

I did mollify him with my words and now he acted like a friendly fuzzy mole.

MOLLIFY
<Mol-lee-fye>

Placate; pacify; appease;
Making someone happy by saying kind things
I will mollify him with good words and he will not be upset.

MOLL - IFY

Moll	(Reminds)	Mole or trickster
Ify	(Reminds)	Iffy

Memory Trick: A mole uses iffy words to make you happy.
MOLE IFFY

I don't know. Caprice means to change your mind on a whim. We will go where you want to go.

I am not afraid to remonstrate you. You do not scare me.

REMONSTRATE
<Re-mon-strayt>
Plead; fight; dispute;
Making an opposing argument.
You remonstrate him and stand up for
yourself.

REMONSTRATE

Remonstrate	(Like)	Demonstrate

Memory Trick: I will demonstrate against
your argument.
DEMONSTRATE

I tell you, "I love your dowdy hat!" Why
don't you thank me?

SEP 23

Coffee is my hedonic pleasure. I allow myself only nine cups a day.

HEDONIC
<He-don-nik>
Pleasurable; decadent; wanton;
Being full of pleasure.
Your hedonic nature pleases me
because you are fun.

HED - ONIC

Hed	(Reminds)	Heady
Onic	(Reminds)	Tonic

Memory Trick: It is like a heady tonic
when we have fun.
HEADY TONIC

Dowdy means to be vulgar looking or to
be in bad taste. I said, "I love your ugly
hat."

A bee will fructify flowers by carrying pollen to other flowers. Flowers use bees to multiply.

FRUCTIFY
<Frook-tee-feye>

Pollinate; fertilize; impregnate;
Bearing fruit.
The bee will fructify the flowers when it
pollinates them.

FRUC - TIFY

Fruc	(Reminds)	Fruit
Tify	(Reminds)	Multiply

Memory Trick: Fruit multiplies.
FRUIT MULTIPLY

A bee does not have hoofs. How does a
bee, behoove you?

SEP 25

He lived in a tent, but the chimney made it appear pretentious. He wanted people to think it was a big house.

39

PRETENTIOUS
<Pre-ten-shush>
Pompous; showy; grandiose
Trying to impress by making something appear grander than it is.
He wore a pretentious watch that looks expensive, but we knew it was cheap.

PRETENT - IOUS

Pretent	(Reminds)	Pretend

Memory Trick: We pretend when we act better than we are.
PRETEND

It makes honey. Behoove means to use or profit from. You benefit when you eat the honey.

The epilogue of the book continued the story and showed a happy ending.

EPILOGUE
<Ep-pee-log>
Postscript; summation; follow-up;
Ending a book with a conclusion.
I added an epilogue and now the reader
knows what happened.

EPI - LOGUE

Epi	(Reminds)	Epic
Logue	(Rhymes)	Log

Memory Trick: An epic log tells us what
happened.
EPIC LOG

You show up on an antedate for a date.
How was your date?

The trophy was a great accolade.

ACCOLADE
<Ak-co-laid>
Praise; applaud; salute
Anything that shows appreciation
The accolade surprised me because I did
not expect everyone to cheer.

ACCOL - ADE

Accol	(Reminds)	Acclaim
Ade	(Reminds)	Ade or a drink

Memory Trick: The acclaim we drink like
Ade because so much is given.
ACLAIM ADE

Not good. Antedate is a date earlier than
a given date. You showed up early and
your date was not there.

The punctilious artist made every paint stroke perfect.

PUNCTILIOUS
<Punk-til-lee-us>
Precise; correct; strict;
Doing something with great care and attention to detail.
I was punctilious with my grammar and my report was excellent.

PUNCT - TILIOUS

Punct	(Reminds)	Punctual
Tilious	(Reminds)	Titillate

Memory Trick: A punctual person is titillated by precision.
PUNCTUAL TITILATE

You are a veracious and ravenous. You say, "You did not eat the pie." I believe you. Why?

I had a prescient feeling and ducked down just in time.

PRESCIENT
<Pres-shent>

Predict; visionary; insight;
Foreseeing events in the future.
The prescient writing astounded us
because everything came true.

PRE - SCIENT

Pre	(Reminds)	Predict
Scient	(Reminds)	Sense

Memory Trick: We can predict because
we have a sense.
PREDICT SENSE

A veracious person tells the truth.
Veracious means having the habit of
being honest.

SEP 30

The gestation ended and soon there were many more rabbits.

GESTATION
<Jes-tay-shun>
Pregnancy; incubation; conception;
Carrying a baby inside a womb.
Her gestation was long and her belly
grew big.

GE - STATION

Ge	(Reminds)	Gee or awe
Station	(Reminds)	Station

Memory Trick: Gee. There is a baby in
the station.
GEE STATION

You go trundling. What do you do with
your balls?

This contract is esoteric. I don't understand it.

ESOTERIC
<Es-o-ter-rik>
Private; exclusive; cryptic;
Only understood with confidential
knowledge.
The trick is esoteric because the secret is
hidden and mystical.

E - SOTERIC

| Soteric | (Reminds) | Secret |

Memory Trick: It is a secret.
SECRET

You throw them down the lane. Trundling
means to bowl.

A cavalcade of clowns rolled by. They were followed by a little car.

CAVALCADE
<Kav-al-kayd>
Procession; caravan; parade;
Moving in a parade on horseback or in cars.
The cavalcade was endless and we admired the horses.

CAVAL - CADE

Caval	(Reminds)	Cavalry
Cade	(Reminds)	Parade

Memory Trick: A cavalry parade goes by us.
CAVALRY PARADE

Is your commorancy common or is it fancy?

OCT 3

I had a presage that I would play in the snow today.

PRESAGE
<Pres-sadge>

Prophecy; forewarning; boding;
Having intuition or foresight.
I have a presage that something good is
going to happen.

PRE - SAGE

Pre	(Reminds)	Before
Sage	(Means)	Sage or psychic

Memory Trick: He knows before it
happens because he is a sage.
PRE SAGE

It depends. A commorancy is the place
where you live or sleep.

The growth food made the flower burgeon before my eyes.

BURGEON
<Bur-gin>
Prosper; blossom; flourish;
Blooming at a great rate.
Your sales will burgeon and grow fast.

BUR - G - EON

Bur	(Reminds)	Of burst
Eon	(Reminds)	Eon or a long time

Memory Trick: It bursts for an eon
because it grows fast.
BURST EON

You come home and realize your brazier
is hot. Why are you happy about it?

IT'S AN AUSPICIOUS DAY,
FOR YOU CAN SEE,
MONEY CAME MY WAY,
AND I WON THE LOTTERY!

AUSPICIOUS
<Or-spish-shus>
Prosperous; favorable; lucky;
Favored by fortune or a new beginning.
This is an auspicious day because I won
the lottery.

AU - SPICIOUS

Au	(Rhymes)	Awe
Spicious	(Reminds)	Delicious

Memory Trick: We are awed by good
fortune and it is delicious.
AWE DELCIOUS

A brazier holds hot coal. Your house is
nice and warm. Pronounced: Bray-zure

All were felicitous.

FELICITOUS
<Fel-lis-set-tus>
Prosperous; jolly; Joyous;
Well apt for a pleasant situation.
You are felicitous because you are
always happy.

FEL - ICITOUS

Fel	(Reminds)	Feel
Icitous	(Reminds)	Delicious

Memory Trick: We feel delicious because
we are happy.
FEEL DELICIOUS

Your eyes belie where your ball lies. Do I
know where your ball is?

The bull was a bulwark against the cat.
The mouse now felt very safe.

BULWARK
<Bull-wark>
Protect; guard; fort;
Fortifying against danger.
The bulwark safeguarded the birds
against the wind of the storm.

BUL - WARK

Bul	(Reminds)	Bull
Wark	(Reminds)	Work

Memory Trick: Protecting is work for a
bull.
BULL WORK

Yes. Your eyes give away where your
ball is. Belie means to reveal a secret.

I realized it was bad to quibble with a cat when I saw the claws come out.

QUIBBLE
<Kwib-bul>

Protest; bicker; disagree;
Verbally fight about unimportant things.
I never quibble because I would rather
talk about real issues.

QUI - BLE

Qui	(Reminds)	Quiz
Ble	(Rhymes)	Bull

Memory Trick: I quiz you like a bull.
QUIZ BULL

You don't like germane things. Why don't
you respond when someone greets you?

OCT 9

DO YOU READ A GAZETTE,
IT HAS NEWS AND MORE,
IF YOU DON'T YOU MAY REGRET,
NOT KNOWING WHAT WAS BEFORE.

GAZETTE
\<Ga-zet\>

Publication; magazine; newspaper;
Proving news as a newspaper or a daily
paper.
I bought a gazette and it had interesting
news in it.

GAZE - ETTE

Gaze	(Reminds)	Gaze or look
Ette	(Reminds)	Vignette or story

Memory Trick: We gaze at the vignette.
GAZE VIGNETTE

Germane means appropriate. You don't
like appropriate things like greeting
people.

OCT 10

The officious woman insisted that I not eat ice cream before dinner. She was always annoying.

OFFICIOUS
<Oh-fish-ish>
Pushy; intrusive; meddling;
Giving unwanted help.
Stop giving officious advice because I
can choose my own shoes.

OFF - ICIOUS

Off	(Reminds)	Off or back off
Icious	(Reminds)	Vicious

Memory Trick: Back off with your advice
or I will be vicious.
OFF VICIOUS

Your car has a stalwart engine. Can you
drive it or does it stall?

I CANNOT SOLVE IT,

IT WILL ADDLE ME,

I DON'T HAVE THE WIT,

A PUZZLE IT WILL BE.

ADDLE
<Ah-del>

Puzzle; baffle; muddle;
Confused.
The puzzle will addle me because I
cannot figure it out.

ADD - LE

Add	(Reminds)	Add
Le	(Reminds)	Less

Memory Trick: It adds up less when we
are confused.
ADD LESS

You can drive it. Stalwart means being
strong. Your car has a strong engine.

My cat must always be thirsty because he always seems to need to slake his thirst.

SLAKE
<Slayke>
Quench; refresh; satisfy;
Quenching thirst.
Slake your thirst and you will please your
parched throat.

S - LAKE

Lake	(Reminds)	Lake

Memory Trick: A lake will satisfy your
thirst.
LAKE

Tonight, I will lock my doors and
lucubrate for hours. What am I doing?

He was a bibliophile and constantly read books.

BIBLIOPHILE
<Bib-lee-oh-file>
Reader; scholar; intellectual;
Loving books.
You are a bibliophile because you have many books.

BIBLIO - PHILE

Biblio	(Reminds)	Book
Phile	(Means)	Lover of

Memory Trick: Book lover.
BOOK LOVER

Studying. Lucubrate means to work or study at night.

I found that a stick is the best way to hamper a snake.

HAMPER
\<Ham-per\>

Refrain; obstruct; curb;
Hinder by blocking.
Hamper the dog by closing the gate and he can't get out.

HAMPER

Hamper	(Reminds)	Hamper or box

Memory Trick: It is in a hamper and it is blocked.

HAMPER

A cetacean swims by our boat. Why are we not afraid?

OCT 15

*The only vestiges of the loaf of bread
were some breadcrumbs.*

VESTIGE
<Ves-tidge>
Relic; remnant; remains;
Existing now only in pieces of evidence.
A pyramid is a vestige of a great
civilization.

VEST - IGE

Vest	(Reminds)	Invest
Ige	(Reminds)	Age

Memory Trick: Invested over the ages
and gone.
INVEST AGE

A cetacean is a dolphin or a whale.
Cetacean means an aquatic mammal
having a blowhole.

OCT 16

I put a carrot out to appease the rabbit so it would stop eating my flowers.

APPEASE
<Ah-pees>
Relieve; placate; soothe;
Creating a feeling of peace and calm.
I gave a life vest to appease him and he
no longer worried.

APP - EASE

App	(Reminds)	Applaud
Ease	(Means)	Ease or make better

Memory Trick: We applaud when
something is eased.
APPLAUD EASE

You cogitate loafs of bread. What will you
probably do next?

YOU GIVE UP YOUR CROWN WHEN YOU ABDICATE

ABDICATE
<Ab-dee-kayt>
Relinquish; step down; cede;
Resigning from a position.
He will abdicate his throne and resign in
the morning.

AB - DICATE

Ab	(Reminds)	Absolve
Dictate	(Reminds)	Dictator

Memory Trick: Absolve from being a
dictator.
ABSOLVE DICTATOR

Think about something more interesting.
Cogitate means to think deeply. Thinking
about bread is boring.

WHEN YOU ABJURE,
YOU QUIT YOUR CLUB,
BETTER BE SURE,
YOU'RE NOT MAKING A FLUB.

ABJURE
<Ab-jur>
Repudiate; reject; disavow;
Abandoning an oath.
Members can abjure allegiance and give
up their club membership.

AB - JURE

Ab	(Reminds)	Abdicate
Jure	(Reminds)	Jerk

Memory Trick: We abdicate and jerk
away.
ABDICATE JERK

California is not caliginous. How can that
be?

I could not find a denizen in sight.

DENIZEN
<Den-ne-zen>
Resident; citizen; occupant;
Living as a dweller in a habitat.
The denizen greeted us and opened the gate.

DEN - IZEN

Den	(Reminds)	Den or a room
Izen	(Reminds)	Citizen

Memory Trick: A citizen dwells in a room.
DEN CITIZEN

California is bright and sunny. Caliginous means being dark and gloomy.

OCT 20

I TAKE A GOOD REPOSE,
AND GET A LOT OF SLEEP,
PAJAMAS ARE MY CLOTHES,
IN CASE I'M COUNTING SHEEP.

REPOSE
<Re-poze>
Rest; slumber; rest;
Resting in a peaceful position.
I will take my repose and wake in an
hour.

RE - POSE

Re	(Reminds)	Return or again
Pose	(Reminds)	Pose or still

Memory Trick: I return to a pose and I am
not awake.
RETURN POSE

We play scrabble. You want to quit. I say
quitting is an obliquity thing to do. Why do
you sit back down and play?

Let me paraphrase it this way. You won the lottery!

PARAPHRASE
<Pa-ra-fraze>

Restate; recap; reword;
Rewording something to clarify it.
Let me paraphrase because I can explain
it better.

PARA - PHRASE

Para	(Reminds)	Parable
Phrase	(Reminds)	Phrase or say

Memory Trick: Saying a parable story as
a new phrase.
PARABLE PHRASE

Obliquity means dishonest or
underhanded.

He had an afflatus and never knew why he painted a cat.

AFFLATUS
<Ah-flat-tus>
Revelation; vision; insight;
Getting a creative impulse.
I had an afflatus and I created a new
style of painting.

AFFLAT - US

Afflat	(Reminds)	Inflate
Us	(Reminds)	Us

Memory Trick: Inflate us with inspiration.
INFLATE US

You get in your car and forgo a road trip.
How was your trip?

OCT 23

The robot wanted to venerate the soda machine. He seemed to think it was the robot leader.

VENERATE
<Ven-ah-rayte>
Reverence; cherish; adore;
Admiring or holding in the highest regard.
The readers venerate a good book
because a good story is always loved.

VENE - RATE

Vene	(Reminds)	Vent or say a lot
Rate	(Reminds)	Rate

Memory Trick: I vent a good rate for you.
VENT RATE

You never took it. Forgo means to give
up or to not do.

Carrots are the antithesis of carrot cake, but we both enjoyed our dishes.

ANTITHESIS
<Ant-tith-ee-sis>
Reverse; counter; contrast;
Contrasting against something.
Big is the antithesis of small because it is
the exact opposite.

ANTI - THESIS

Anti	(Reminds)	Anti
Thesis	(Reminds)	Thesis or essay

Memory Trick: The anti-thesis is the
opposite.
ANTI THESIS

You abrade the hair on a tiger. What
should you do next?

We were surprised to learn he was propertied and he donated large amounts of land.

PROPERTIED
<Prop-per-teed>
Rich; wealthy; prosperous;
Rich and owning land
You will be propertied and have a lot of
money.

PROPERTIE - D

Propertie	(Reminds)	Property

Memory Trick: A rich person owns
property.
PROPERTY

Run! Abrade means to scrape off or wear
down by rubbing.

Wearing shorts with a flowered shirt was not apropos because it was a fancy party.

APROPOS
<Ap-pro-po>
Right; correct timing; suitable;
Timing that is good and appropriate.
Your comments are apropos because
kind words are appropriate.

A - PRO - POS

Pro	(Reminds)	Proper
Pos	(Reminds)	Positive

Memory Trick: It was a proper and
positive thing to say.
PROPER POSITIVE

You are a sailboat captain. You yell, "Put
up the sails and scuttle ahead!" How fast
do you go?

*The commodious house stood before us.
Even the door was huge.*

COMMODIOUS
<Kom-mowd-dee-us>
Roomy; big; grand;
A place that is spacious.
The commodious house loomed large
and the windows glimmered.

COMM - ODIOUS

Comm	(Reminds)	Common
Odious	(Reminds)	Odor or smells

Memory Trick: A common space is filled
with odors.
COMMON ODOR

You don't. You sink your boat. Scuttle
means to sink a ship on purpose.

CPSIA information can be obtained at www.ICGtesting.com
Printed in the USA
LVOW04s1600080215

426179LV00030B/1481/P

9 781499 273137